31 Days of Leadership with Nehemiah: A Devotional for School Leaders

Dr. Tenry D. Berry

BK Royston Publishing
Jeffersonville, IN 47131
http://www.bkroystonpublishing.com
bkroystonpublishing@gmail.com

© Copyright – 2025

All Rights Reserved. No part of this book may be reproduced, stored in a retrieval system, or transmitted by any means without the written permission of the author.

ISBN: 978-1-967282-80-7

New International Version NIV - Holy Bible, New International Version®, NIV® Copyright ©1973, 1978, 1984, 2011 by Biblica, Inc.® Used by permission. All rights reserved worldwide.

Printed in the United States of America

Dedication

To my parents, **Henry and Patricia Berry**
Though you now rest in eternity, your love, wisdom, and belief in the power of education are the foundation upon which I stand. You fueled my ambition, guided my steps, and inspired me to finish what I started. This book is a reflection of the seeds you planted in me.

To my wife, **Paige**
My encourager, my steady place, my greatest cheerleader. Thank you for pushing me when I felt tired, speaking life when I needed strength, and believing in this dream from the very beginning. Your love made this possible.

To my children, **Kendahl, Khloe, and Kingston**
You see me as a hero, and you make me want to be one. Your joy, curiosity, and unwavering belief in me gave my heart the fuel to finish strong. You inspire me to dream bigger, lead better, and walk in purpose boldly. This is for you, too.

To every school leader who rises each day with a burden for students and a vision for their future. May you find strength, wisdom, and courage in the God who called you to this sacred work.

Special Thanks

A heartfelt expression of gratitude to
Dr. C. L. Roberts

Thank you for your constant push, voice of encouragement, and unwavering belief in my ability to finish what I started. Your sermon series and Bible studies through the book of Nehemiah stirred something deep within me; awakening vision, sharpening purpose, and igniting the fire that led to the creation of this devotional. I am grateful for your leadership, your obedience to God, and the example you set for all who follow your teaching.

Foreword By Dr. C. L. Roberts

For more than twenty years, I have had the honor of walking alongside Dr. Tenry D. Berry—as a friend, a fellow laborer in the Kingdom, and as a leader who carries a rare grace for both the classroom and the sanctuary. I have watched him lead students, staff, and congregations with the steady heart of a servant and the sharp mind of a strategist. He is, in every sense, a teacher's teacher and a leader's leader.

When Dr. Berry shared that God had stirred his heart through my own preaching and Bible studies on Nehemiah, and that those moments helped ignite the vision for this book, I felt both humbled and grateful. What you now hold in your hands is evidence that when the Word of God meets a prepared, disciplined life, something powerful is born.

This devotional is not theory on leadership—it is lived leadership wrapped in Scripture. Over the course of 31 days, Dr. Berry walks school leaders through a journey that is as practical as it is prophetic. Each day is intentionally structured with a Scripture, reflection, leadership insight, affirmation, prayer, and life application.

From the very first week, "The Anchor Point: Grounding Leadership in Students," you can feel Dr. Berry's heart as both an educator and a shepherd. On Day 1, when he talks about Nehemiah weeping over the broken walls and ties that image to the "broken walls" in the lives of students—hungry children, struggling families, and students falling behind—he frames leadership as more than a job. He calls it what it truly is: a holy burden.

Later, in Day 18, when he highlights Nehemiah's response, "I am doing a great work and cannot come down," and applies it to the distractions that crowd a school leader's schedule, he gives you not only inspiration but language and focus. That single sentence alone will preach to your calendar, your inbox, and your boundaries.

Throughout "The Greenhouse Effect," "Time and Truth," and "Brave Presence," Dr. Berry weaves together prayer, emotional intelligence, instructional leadership, culture-building, justice, and stewardship. He reminds school leaders that compassion is courage, prayer is preparation, delegation is multiplication, and celebration is fuel.

But what stands out most is that Dr. Berry writes as someone who has truly been there. His reflections read like they were written after long nights, weighty decisions, and holy burdens. His voice is one of both tenderness and truth—a combination every leader needs.

To every school leader who walks through these pages: Let Nehemiah's story remind you that God sees the broken places you are called to rebuild. Let the affirmations sharpen how you speak about your assignment. Let the prayers and life applications pull these lessons into the real spaces you lead every day.

You are stewarding futures. You are guarding gateways to destiny. You are, indeed, doing a great work.

It is with deep joy and honor that I commend to you ***"31 Days of Leadership with Nehemiah."*** My prayer is that your heart will be steadied, your hands strengthened, and your leadership renewed.

May your walls be rebuilt. May your courage be restored. May your leadership finish well.

Dr. C. L. Roberts Senior Pastor
Kingdom Impact Center
Valdosta, Georgia

Table of Contents

Dedication	iii
Special Thanks	iv
Foreword	v
Introduction	xiii
How to Use this Devotional	xv
Word of Encouragement	xvii
Week 1 – The Anchor Point: Grounding Leadership in Students	1
Day 1: Feeling the Burden	3
Day 2: Seeking God First	7
Day 3: Leading with Humility	11
Day 4: A Heart for the Mission	15
Day 5: Courage to Act	19
Day 6: Recognizing God's Favor	23
Day 7: Vision and Planning	27
Week 2 - The Greenhouse Effect: Growing People in Every Season	31
Day 8: Rallying the People	33
Day 9: Facing Opposition Together	37

Day 10: Watchfulness in Coaching	41
Day 11: Building Unity	45
Day 12: Confronting Fear with Courage	49
Day 13: Leading by Example	53
Day 14: Delegating Responsibility	57
Week 3 - Time and Truth: Mastering Minutes and Hard Conversations	61
Day 15: Renewed Strength for the Work	63
Day 16: Confronting Injustice Without Delay	67
Day 17: Personal Sacrifice in Leadership	71
Day 18: Staying Focused Amid Distractions	75
Day 19: Praying for Strength	79
Day 20: Celebrating Victories	83
Day 21: Leading with Integrity	87
Weeks 4 and 5 - Brave Presence: Showing up and Speaking up!	91
Day 22: Empowering Others	93
Day 23: Living with Accountability	97
Day 24: Joy in Obedience	101
Day 25: Confession and Renewal	105

Day 26: Remembering God's Faithfulness	109
Day 27: Renewing Commitments	113
Day 28: Stewardship of Resources	117
Day 29: Guarding Against Compromise	121
Day 30: Trusting God with the Future	125
Day 31: Finishing Well	129
About the Author	133

Introduction

Leadership is both a gift and a burden. As school leaders, we bear the responsibility of shaping futures, guiding teachers, fostering culture, and ensuring that students have the opportunity to thrive. It is a calling that stretches far beyond academic achievement. Leadership touches lives, families, and communities.

In the Bible, Nehemiah stands out as a leader who carried a holy burden. He wept over the broken walls of Jerusalem, prayed earnestly, and then courageously led the people to rebuild. He faced opposition, navigated conflict, managed resources, and ultimately finished his assignment well. Nehemiah's leadership story is not just ancient history—it is a timeless blueprint for leaders today.

This devotional is designed for school leaders who desire to lead with both professional excellence and spiritual depth. Over the course of thirty-one days, you will:

- **Reflect** on Scripture and biblical leadership principles.

- **Learn** from Nehemiah's example as well as other leaders in Scripture.

- **Apply** practical insights through the lens of school leadership.

- **Align** your leadership with effective school leadership habits.

- **Grow** in leadership competencies, subtly woven throughout each reflection.

Each day includes a Scripture, reflection, leadership insight, affirmation, prayer, and life application. The reflections are written from the perspective of an experienced school leader and minister, offering both spiritual encouragement and practical wisdom.

How to Use This Devotional

- **Read one devotional each day.** Take time to meditate on the Scripture and reflect on how it applies to your leadership.

- **Pray the prayer provided.** Let it guide your conversations with God about your school, your staff, and your students.

- **Speak the daily affirmation.** Declare truth over your leadership and let it reshape your mindset.

- **Complete the life application.** In the workbook edition, space is provided for journaling. Use it honestly and specifically to apply what you are learning to your own context.

- **Invite accountability.** Consider working through this devotional with another leader or a small group of colleagues. Discuss your insights and encourage one another in the journey.

This devotional is not meant to be rushed. It is designed to form a rhythm of reflection, prayer, and action. My prayer is that as you walk with Nehemiah for thirty-one days, you will be reminded that leadership is not simply a role—it is a calling. And the God who called you is faithful to equip you.

A Word of Encouragement

You are not leading alone. Just as God strengthened Nehemiah's hands to rebuild Jerusalem's walls, He will strengthen yours. The challenges before you may seem significant, but the God within you is greater. This is your season to lead with vision, courage, humility, and faith.

Let us begin.

Week 1

The Anchor Point: Grounding Leadership in Students

Day 1: Feeling the Burden

Scripture: Nehemiah 1:3-4 (NIV)
They said to me, "Those who survived the exile and are back in the province are in great trouble and disgrace. The wall of Jerusalem is broken down, and its gates have been burned with fire." When I heard these things, I sat down and wept. For some days I mourned and fasted and prayed before the God of heaven.

Reflection: When Nehemiah heard the report of Jerusalem's broken walls and burned gates, he sat down, wept, and prayed. His reaction reveals the heart of a true leader who allows the suffering of others to become personal. He did not dismiss the news as someone else's problem, but he took ownership in prayer and intercession. Jeremiah, often referred to as the weeping prophet, carried a similar burden because he grieved over Israel's disobedience (Jeremiah 9:1). Jesus also wept over Jerusalem, moved with compassion for people who choose not to receive the peace of God offered to them (Luke 19:41-42).

Leadership that does not feel deeply for the people it serves will eventually grow cold and mechanical.

In schools, we must allow the "broken walls" of our students' lives to move us to action. Broken walls may appear to be students falling behind academically, children arriving at school hungry, or families struggling without support. A leader who experiences this burden cannot remain passive. They will engage families, rally resources, and raise expectations so that no child is overlooked. Schools thrive when leaders cultivate high expectations for all students and encourage strong involvement from parents and the community.

Nehemiah lived this truth, not by simply giving orders, but by engaging the whole community in a shared mission.

Leadership Insight: Compassion is not weakness. It is the foundation of courageous action.

Affirmation: *"I respond to the needs of students with compassion and purpose."*

Prayer: Lord, allow me to see my students as You see them. Break my heart for what breaks Yours and cause me to act with courage and love.

Life Application: Identify a "broken wall" in your school. Then write a prayer petitioning God to give you wisdom and strength to address it in love.

Life Application

_____
_____
_____
_____
_____
_____
_____
_____
_____
_____
_____
_____
_____
_____
_____
_____
_____
_____
_____
_____
_____
_____
_____
_____
_____
_____
_____
_____
_____

Life Application

Day 2: Seeking God First

Scripture: Nehemiah 1:4 (NIV)
When I heard these things, I sat down and wept. For some days I mourned and fasted and prayed before the God of heaven.

Reflection: Before Nehemiah made a plan or spoke to the king, he prayed and fasted. He understood that true wisdom comes from the Lord. Many leaders fall into the trap of rushing ahead with strategies without pausing to seek God's direction. Nehemiah reminds us that leadership is, first and foremost, a spiritual act.

Jesus often withdrew to pray before making significant decisions. Before selecting His twelve disciples, He spent the entire night in prayer (Luke 6:12-13). Before the cross, He prayed in Gethsemane, submitting to the Father's will (Matthew 26:36-39).

Great leaders recognize that their strength is not in their position but in their connection to God.

School leaders face numerous decisions, such as curriculum, personnel, discipline, scheduling, and resource allocation. When those decisions are guided by prayer, they are more likely to reflect what is truly in students' best interest. Clear communication and wise use of time and resources flow from leaders who first bend their knee before the Lord.

Nehemiah demonstrates that prayer is not wasted time, but a preparation that gives power to every decision that follows.

Leadership Insight: Prayer and fasting prepare leaders to act with clarity and courage.

Affirmation: *"I seek God's wisdom before I act."*

Prayer: Lord, daily remind me that my first responsibility is to seek You. Teach me to entirely rely on Your wisdom in every decision I make regarding the well-being of my school and students.

Life Application: Begin tomorrow with five minutes of prayer specifically for your students. Then, ask God for wisdom in one decision you need to make this week.

Life Application

Life Application

Day 3: Leading with Humility

Scripture: Nehemiah 1:6 (NIV)
"let your ear be attentive and your eyes open to hear the prayer your servant is praying before you day and night for your servants, the people of Israel. I confess the sins we Israelites, including myself and my father's family, have committed against you."

Reflection: Nehemiah did not pray as if he were above his people. He confessed his own sins as well as theirs, saying, *"I confess the sins we Israelites, including myself and my father's family, have committed against you."* That is humility in leadership. It takes courage to admit failure, but humility builds the foundation of trust.

David modeled humility when confronted by the prophet Nathan. He did not defend himself but admitted, "I have sinned against the Lord" (2 Samuel 12:13). Daniel also demonstrated it when he prayed a similar prayer of confession on behalf of the nation, including himself in their shortcomings (Daniel 9:4-6).

Leaders who are brave enough to acknowledge their weaknesses demonstrate a strength of character that others respect.

Humility communicates integrity. Staff notice when leaders own mistakes and model learning. Students learn more from a leader who admits, "I was wrong, and this is how I will do better," than from one who insists on perfection. Humility strengthens communication, builds advocacy, and allows decision-making to flow from honesty rather than pride. It keeps us centered on what matters most: students and their growth. Leaders who lead with humility inspire others to follow with trust and respect.

Leadership Insight: Humility is not weakness. It is the soil where trust and growth flourish.

Affirmation: *"I grow stronger as a leader when I walk in humility."*

Prayer: Father, shield me from pride. Help me to lead with honesty and humility, showing others what it means to be a servant-leader.

Life Application: Think of one mistake you have made in leadership. Write down what you learned from it and how you can model that growth for your staff or students.

Life Application

Life Application

Day 4: A Heart for the Mission

Scripture: Nehemiah 1:11 (NIV)
"Lord, let your ear be attentive to the prayer of this your servant and to the prayer of your servants who delight in revering your name. Give your servant success today by granting him favor in the presence of this man."

Reflection: Nehemiah's story begins with prayer. His request was not simply for favor with the king, but for God's strength to serve his people well. Leadership at its core is stewardship, which is a willingness to carry the weight of others. Moses interceded when the people of Israel were on the verge of destruction (Exodus 32:11-14). David cried out to God when his people were suffering (2 Samuel 24:17). Jesus Himself wept over Jerusalem, longing for the people to be gathered in safety (Luke 13:34).

As a school leader, I have learned that before policies are drafted, meetings are held, or strategies are deployed, my heart must be anchored in a deep concern for the best interest of children.

Leadership grounded in prayer and compassion has always been God's pattern.

In our schools, the "walls" we build are not stone, but safety, equity, and a focus on learning. Effective leaders keep the mission in view. The students must be able to learn in an environment where they feel safe, valued, and challenged. This is the kind of leadership research consistently affirms: leaders who keep learning and student well-being at the center of their work have the most significant impact.

Nehemiah shows us that when a leader's heart is aligned with God's mission, vision becomes compelling, communication carries weight, and people follow with confidence. It all begins with the heart.

Leadership Insight: Every decision must be filtered through the question: *"Will this benefit students?"*

Affirmation: *"My leadership begins and ends with what is best for students."*

Prayer: Lord, align my heart with Your mission and with the needs of the students I serve. Give me a shepherd's heart that reflects Your love.

Life Application: Take time today to journal about what breaks your heart for students. How does this burden shape your vision as a leader?

Life Application

Life Application

_____
_____
_____
_____
_____
_____
_____
_____
_____
_____
_____
_____
_____
_____
_____
_____
_____
_____
_____
_____
_____
_____
_____
_____
_____
_____
_____
_____
_____

Day 5: Courage to Act

Scripture: Nehemiah 2:2-3 (NIV)
"so the king asked me, "Why does your face look so sad when you are not ill? This can be nothing but sadness of heart." I was very much afraid, but I said to the king, "May the king live forever! Why should my face not look sad when the city where my ancestors are buried lies in ruins, and its gates have been destroyed by fire?"

Reflection: When Nehemiah approached the king, he took a tremendous risk because expressing sorrow in the king's presence could have cost him his life. Yet he spoke boldly, asking for permission to rebuild Jerusalem's walls. Leadership often requires courage to stand for what is right, even when it comes at personal cost.

Joshua was told, "Be strong and courageous... for the Lord your God will be with you wherever you go" (Joshua 1:9). Esther risked her life by approaching the king to plead for her people (Esther 4:16). Jesus confronted both spiritual and political powers with courage, even knowing it would lead to the cross (Luke 13:31-33).

Leaders who fear risks seldom witness lasting transformation.

For school leaders, courage manifests in advocating for resources, confronting inequities, or making tough decisions that prioritize students' well-being. At times, it may mean saying no to distractions or yes to changes that others resist. Courageous leaders keep the mission clear: what benefits students must take precedence over what is convenient.

Nehemiah shows us that courage is not recklessness. It is faith that God's hand is at work and that He will provide favor for the mission He has assigned.

Leadership Insight: Courageous leadership puts students' well-being above convenience or comfort.

Affirmation: *"I lead with courage for the sake of my students."*

Prayer: Father, give me boldness to act when action is required. Let me stand firmly for what is right, even when it is costly.

Life Application: Identify one decision you have been hesitant to make for your students. Write down the first step you can take to build courage this week.

Life Application

Life Application

Day 6: Recognizing God's Favor

Scripture: Nehemiah 2:4-8(NIV)
"The king said to me, "What is it you want?" Then I prayed to the God of heaven, and I answered the king, "If it pleases the king and if your servant has found favor in his sight, let him send me to the city in Judah where my ancestors are buried so that I can rebuild it." Then the king, with the queen sitting beside him, asked me, "How long will your journey take, and when will you get back?" It pleased the king to send me; so I set a time. I also said to him, "If it pleases the king, may I have letters to the governors of Trans-Euphrates, so that they will provide me safe-conduct until I arrive in Judah? And may I have a letter to Asaph, keeper of the royal park, so he will give me timber to make beams for the gates of the citadel by the temple and for the city wall and for the residence I will occupy?" And because the gracious hand of my God was on me, the king granted my requests.

Reflection: Nehemiah prayed for favor, and God answered. The king not only permitted him to go but also provided letters, safe passage, and resources. This was more than a political strategy. It was divine provision. Joseph found favor in Egypt, from Potiphar to Pharaoh (Genesis 39:21, 41:39-41). Daniel found favor in Babylon, rising to influence through God's wisdom (Daniel 1:9, 2:48). Jesus Himself grew in favor with God and man (Luke 2:52). When God grants favor, doors open that no one can shut.

As leaders, we must recognize that opportunities, resources, and partnerships are gifts from God. They are not simply the result of networking or strategy. They are blessings to be managed well. In schools, this may manifest as unexpected grants, supportive community partnerships, or timely staff additions. The question is, how do we use these provisions?

Leaders who steward resources wisely build credibility and ensure students receive the best possible opportunities.

Nehemiah teaches us that favor is not the finish line but the starting point. Once God provides, leaders must act with responsibility and care.

Leadership Insight: Opportunities are not luck. They are God's provision, entrusted to leaders for the good of others.

Affirmation: *"I recognize God's favor and steward it well for my students."*

Prayer: Thank You, Lord, for the opportunities and resources You have provided. Help me use them wisely for students' growth and safety.

Life Application: Reflect on one recent blessing or opportunity in your leadership. Write down how it can directly benefit students and how you will steward it well.

Life Application

Life Application

Day 7: Vision and Planning

Scripture: Nehemiah 2:11-16 (NIV)
"I went to Jerusalem, and after staying there three days I set out during the night with a few others. I had not told anyone what my God had put in my heart to do for Jerusalem. There were no mounts with me except the one I was riding on. By night I went out through the Valley Gate toward the Jackal[a] Well and the Dung Gate, examining the walls of Jerusalem, which had been broken down, and its gates, which had been destroyed by fire. Then I moved on toward the Fountain Gate and the King's Pool, but there was not enough room for my mount to get through; so I went up the valley by night, examining the wall. Finally, I turned back and reentered through the Valley Gate. The officials did not know where I had gone or what I was doing, because as yet I had said nothing to the Jews or the priests or nobles or officials or any others who would be doing the work."

Reflection: Before announcing his plan, Nehemiah inspected the walls. He understood that vision must be paired with careful planning. A dream without a plan remains a dream, but a vision anchored in prayer and strategy becomes reality.

Joseph had dreams of leadership, but he also developed administrative skills that saved nations from famine (Genesis 41:46-49). Jesus had a clear mission and prepared His disciples with teaching, mentoring, and sending them in pairs (Luke 10:1).

Great leaders do not simply inspire. They equip, organize, and guide.

A vision for student success must be more than words on a poster. It must translate into instructional guidance, resource allocation, and clear communication. A leader's ability to inspect the "walls" and honestly assess the current state creates credibility and focus. This is where vision becomes actionable.

Nehemiah's planning gave the people confidence to join him in rebuilding. Leaders who combine faith, vision, and strategy create momentum that inspires others to give their best.

Leadership Insight: Vision is only as strong as the plan that supports it.

Affirmation: *"I am a visionary leader who plans with wisdom and clarity."*

Prayer: Lord, guide my vision and sharpen my planning. Let my words and actions inspire others to build with purpose.

Life Application: Write down one student-centered initiative you feel called to lead. List three practical steps you can take to bring it closer to reality.

Life Application

Life Application

Week 2
The Greenhouse Effect: Growing People in Every Season

Day 8: Rallying the People

Scripture: Nehemiah 2:17(NIV)
"Then I said to them, "You see the trouble we are in: Jerusalem lies in ruins, and its gates have been burned with fire. Come, let us rebuild the wall of Jerusalem, and we will no longer be in disgrace."

Reflection: After surveying the walls, Nehemiah gathered the people and declared, *"You see the trouble we are in… Come, let us rebuild the wall of Jerusalem, and we will no longer be in disgrace."* His words ignited a movement. Coaching as a leader begins with inspiring people to see what they can accomplish together.

Moses rallied Israel to move forward when they faced the Red Sea (Exodus 14:13-14). Joshua charged the people before they crossed into the promised land (Joshua 1:10-11). Jesus inspired fishermen to leave their nets, promising, *"Follow Me, and I will make you fishers of men"* (Matthew 4:19).

True leaders call people into a vision greater than themselves.

As a school leader, this means painting a clear picture of what success can look like for students and staff. Teachers need encouragement that their labor is not in vain. Families need to believe they are partners in a larger mission. Research shows that when leaders communicate vision with conviction, they strengthen school culture and collective efficacy.

Nehemiah's coaching was not about cheerleading alone. It was about reminding people of God's hand at work and calling them to commit. Leaders who coach relentlessly inspire action, not just applause.

Leadership Insight: Coaching begins with a vision that inspires others to believe and build.

Affirmation: *"I inspire others with vision and conviction."*

Prayer: Lord, grant me the wisdom to encourage those I lead and the courage to call them into greater purpose.

Life Application: Take 5 minutes this week to verbally share one story with your staff that highlights how the school's vision positively impacted a student. Use it as a reminder that students remain at the heart of your leadership.

Life Application

Life Application

Day 9: Facing Opposition Together

Scripture: Nehemiah 4:1-3(NIV)
"When Sanballat heard that we were rebuilding the wall, he became angry and was greatly incensed. He ridiculed the Jews, and in the presence of his associates and the army of Samaria, he said, "What are those feeble Jews doing? Will they restore their wall? Will they offer sacrifices? Will they finish in a day? Can they bring the stones back to life from those heaps of rubble—burned as they are?" Tobiah the Ammonite, who was at his side, said, "What they are building—even a fox climbing up on it would break down their wall of stones!"

Reflection: As soon as Nehemiah began to work, opposition arose. Sanballat mocked and Tobiah ridiculed, saying even a fox could topple their wall. Moses faced constant grumbling in the wilderness, yet reminded Israel of God's promises (Numbers 14:8-9). Paul encouraged Timothy to endure hardship like a good soldier of Christ (2 Timothy 2:3). Jesus warned His disciples that they would face persecution but told them to *"take heart, for I have overcome the world"* (John 16:33).

Coaching requires helping people stand firm in the face of ridicule or resistance.

In schools, opposition may manifest as criticism, resistance to change, or a lack of resources. When leaders coach their teams through opposition, they turn challenges into moments of growth. This requires resilience, encouragement, and constant communication. Staff who see their leader standing firm are more likely to keep building with confidence.

Nehemiah did not let ridicule halt his progress. He prayed, posted guards, and encouraged the people to keep working. Coaching relentlessly means helping others see opposition not as a stop sign but as confirmation that they are building something worthwhile.

Leadership Insight: Resilient leaders coach teams through resistance with faith and focus.

Affirmation: *"I face opposition with courage and help others do the same."*

Prayer: Lord, strengthen my hands and my words so that I may encourage others to stand firm when the work is tested.

Life Application: Write about one area where your team is facing resistance. How can you coach them to respond with resilience instead of retreat?

Life Application

Life Application

Day 10: Watchfulness in Coaching

Scripture: Nehemiah 4:9 (NIV)
"But we prayed to our God and posted a guard day and night to meet this threat."

Reflection: When his enemies threatened, Nehemiah and the people prayed and set guards. His coaching combined spiritual vigilance with practical strategy. Coaching requires both encouragement and watchfulness, ensuring that those we lead are protected from distraction and harm.

Jesus told His disciples, *"Watch and pray so that you will not fall into temptation"* (Matthew 26:41). Paul warned the Ephesian elders to be shepherds who watch over the flock, guarding against wolves (Acts 20:28-29).

> ***Leaders who coach must inspire and guard the mission.***

For school leaders, this may involve monitoring instruction, maintaining a watchful eye on school culture, or shielding staff from unnecessary burdens. It means ensuring that the focus on students remains sharp, even when outside pressures arise. Effective leaders create structures that support staff while maintaining a clear mission.

Nehemiah teaches us that vigilance is a form of care. Coaching relentlessly means urging people forward but also watching over them with prayer and practical support.

Leadership Insight: Effective coaching strikes a balance between encouragement and watchfulness to protect the mission.

Affirmation: *"I watch and pray, guiding with wisdom and care."*

Prayer: Lord, help me to be alert as I lead. Teach me to combine encouragement with discernment so that my team remains strong and resilient.

Life Application: Write one area where your team may be vulnerable. How can you increase vigilance while still inspiring confidence?

Life Application

Life Application

Day 11: Building Unity

Scripture: Nehemiah 4:13 (NIV)
"Therefore I stationed some of the people behind the lowest points of the wall at the exposed places, posting them by families, with their swords, spears and bows."

Reflection: Nehemiah positioned families together to defend and build. This created a natural unity because people worked alongside those they loved and cared for. Jesus prayed for His disciples, *"That they may be one just as you and I are one"* (John 17:21). Paul reminded the Corinthians that the body has many parts. Still, one purpose (1 Corinthians 12:12). Unity is a spiritual principle that multiplies effectiveness.

Coaching means cultivating unity that strengthens the whole.

Unity is essential. A fractured staff cannot carry out a shared mission, but a unified staff can overcome obstacles. Leaders coach toward unity by fostering collaboration, celebrating successes, and reminding people of the larger vision. When people feel they are part of something greater than themselves, their commitment deepens.

Nehemiah understood that unity was both a strategy and a source of strength. Families working together meant morale stayed high and defense was stronger. Leaders who coach relentlessly invest time in cultivating a spirit of togetherness.

Leadership Insight: Coaching fosters unity, transforming individuals into a cohesive team.

Affirmation: *"I cultivate unity and strengthen my team through encouragement."*

Prayer: Lord, help me to build unity among those I lead. Let my words and actions draw people together for a shared purpose.

Life Application: Intentionally invite two staff members who do not typically work together to collaborate on a small task, and publicly celebrate their teamwork.

Life Application

Life Application

Day 12: Confronting Fear with Courage

Scripture: Nehemiah 4:14 (NIV)
"After I looked things over, I stood up and said to the nobles, the officials and the rest of the people, "Don't be afraid of them. Remember the Lord, who is great and awesome, and fight for your families, your sons and your daughters, your wives and your homes."

Reflection: When the people grew fearful, Nehemiah reminded them of God's greatness and the importance of their families. Coaching sometimes means reminding people why they cannot quit.

Joshua told Israel to be strong and courageous because the Lord was with them (Joshua 1:9). David encouraged Solomon to be strong as he prepared to build the temple (1 Chronicles 28:20). Jesus reminded His disciples that though they would face tribulation, His victory was already secure (John 16:33).

Leaders who coach provide courage when fear threatens to hinder progress.

At the school level, fear may manifest as staff feeling overwhelmed by challenges or students questioning their ability to succeed.

A leader's voice can shift the atmosphere by speaking faith, courage, and possibility. This is why leaders must remain anchored in God's promises.

Nehemiah coached his people by pointing their eyes back to God's greatness. Leaders who do the same inspire teams to overcome fear with faith.

Leadership Insight: Coaching gives courage to those tempted by fear or discouragement.

Affirmation: *"I replace fear with faith and help others do the same."*

Prayer: Lord, when fear rises among my team, let my words bring courage. Help me to point them back to Your strength.

Life Application: Reflect on one area where fear is holding your team back. Write a declaration of faith that you can speak over them.

Life Application

Life Application

Day 13: Leading by Example

Scripture: Nehemiah 4:15-16 (NIV)
"When our enemies heard that we were aware of their plot and that God had frustrated it, we all returned to the wall, each to our own work. From that day on, half of my men did the work, while the other half were equipped with spears, shields, bows and armor. The officers posted themselves behind all the people of Judah.."

Reflection: Nehemiah did not simply assign tasks. He worked alongside the people, showing them that leadership is service. His presence communicated, *"We are in this together."* That is the essence of coaching: leading by example.

Jesus demonstrated this when He washed His disciples' feet, saying, *"I have given you an example to follow that you should do as I have done for you"* (John 13:15). Paul echoed this principle when he urged believers to follow him as he followed Christ (1 Corinthians 11:1).

> ***Great leaders model the very work they expect from others.***

In schools, this means principals who visit classrooms, work with teachers, and demonstrate the practices they ask staff to adopt. When leaders embody a strong work ethic, staff are more likely to follow suit. It also builds credibility, showing that leaders understand the realities of the work, not just the theory.

Coaching relentlessly requires presence. It is not enough to point toward the goal. Leaders must step onto the field with their teams. Nehemiah's hands-on leadership inspired the people to labor with renewed strength.

Leadership Insight: Leaders who model hard work create teams that give their best.

Affirmation: *"I lead by example, showing the way through action."*

Prayer: Father, let my example encourage those around me. May my actions inspire my team to serve with diligence and joy.

Life Application: Reflect on one area where you can step in and model the standard you expect from your staff.

Life Application

Life Application

Day 14: Delegating Responsibility

Scripture: Nehemiah 4:19-20 (NIV)
"Then I said to the nobles, the officials and the rest of the people, "The work is extensive and spread out, and we are widely separated from each other along the wall. Wherever you hear the sound of the trumpet, join us there. Our God will fight for us!"

Reflection: Nehemiah knew he could not do everything himself. He appointed teams and assigned them specific responsibilities, ensuring the work continued to be done effectively. Coaching involves trusting others with responsibility and equipping them to succeed.

Moses' father-in-law advised him to delegate so he would not wear himself out (Exodus 18:17-23). Jesus sent out the seventy-two in pairs, entrusting them with ministry (Luke 10:1). Paul instructed Timothy to entrust what he had learned to faithful people who could teach others (2 Timothy 2:2).

Leaders who coach well multiply impact by empowering others to carry the load.

Delegation is essential for sustainability in schools. Leaders who try to carry everything alone quickly burn out. Coaching others by giving them meaningful responsibilities not only lightens the load but also develops the team's capacity. Staff grow when they are trusted and supported in their leadership.

Nehemiah modeled trust by empowering others. Leaders today must do the same if they want to build schools that last.

Leadership Insight: Delegation is not a weakness. It is wisdom that develops others.

Affirmation: *"I empower others by sharing responsibility and trust."*

Prayer: Lord, teach me to trust others with responsibility. Help me to coach them toward growth and success.

Life Application: Write one responsibility you can delegate this week and how you will support the person as they carry it.

Life Application

Life Application

Week 3
Time and Truth: Mastering Minutes and Hard Conversations

Day 15: Renewed Strength for the Work

Scripture: Nehemiah 4:21 (NIV)
"So we continued the work with half the men holding spears, from the first light of dawn till the stars came out."

Reflection: The builders worked tirelessly, from the rising of the sun until the stars appeared. Yet their strength was not only physical, it was spiritual. They pressed forward because their purpose was clear. Isaiah reminds us, *"Those who wait on the Lord will renew their strength; they will soar on wings like eagles"* (Isaiah 40:31).

As leaders, our schedules can quickly overtake us with endless demands.

But purpose brings clarity. When we fix our eyes on the mission, time becomes less about being busy and more about being fruitful. Paul told the Corinthians to "stand firm" and give themselves fully to the work of the Lord, knowing their labor was not in vain (1 Corinthians 15:58).

As school leaders, we often face the temptation to be consumed with urgent but lesser matters. Nehemiah reminds us that lasting work requires discipline, endurance in prayer, and prioritization. Leaders who model diligence without losing focus communicate to staff that perseverance is possible.

Leadership Insight: Strength comes from clarity of purpose and time invested in what matters most.

Affirmation: *"I am renewed daily by God's strength for the work before me."*

Prayer: Lord, renew my energy and remind me that my labor for You and for students is not in vain.

Life Application: Pause during a busy moment this week, take a deep breath, and pray silently: "Lord, give me strength for this task." Allow that moment to reset your spirit before moving forward.

Life Application

Life Application

Day 16: Confronting Injustice Without Delay

Scripture: Nehemiah 5:6-7 (NIV)
"When I heard their outcry and these charges, I was very angry. I pondered them in my mind and then accused the nobles and officials. I told them, "You are charging your own people interest!" So I called together a large meeting to deal with them..."

Reflection: When Nehemiah learned that wealthy Jews were exploiting their poorer brothers through debt and slavery, he did not ignore the issue. He paused, considered, and then acted with boldness to confront the injustice.

> *Leaders must not allow their schedules to push aside what is right.*

Jesus overturned the tables of money changers who exploited worshippers (Matthew 21:12-13). Amos called out those who oppressed the poor and trampled the needy (Amos 5:11-12). Paul rebuked Peter when his actions threatened the truth of the gospel (Galatians 2:11-14). Leaders who prioritize justice, even when inconvenient, reflect God's heart.

In schools, leaders are called to confront inequities in instruction, discipline, and access to opportunities. It is easy to put off tough conversations when the schedule feels too packed. But justice cannot wait. Coaching teachers and advocating for students means courageously addressing wrongs, regardless of how busy the day may be.

Nehemiah teaches us that disciplined leadership is not just about time management. It is about aligning time with God's priorities.

Leadership Insight: Leaders must make time to confront what is wrong and uphold what is right.

Affirmation: *"I create space in my leadership to lead with justice and integrity."*

Prayer: Lord, give me the courage to confront what is wrong in my school and the wisdom to act with fairness and love.

Life Application: Write about one area of injustice in your school that needs your attention.

Life Application

Life Application

Day 17: Personal Sacrifice in Leadership

Scripture: Nehemiah 5:14-15 (NIV)
"Moreover, from the twentieth year of King Artaxerxes, when I was appointed to be their governor in the land of Judah, until his thirty-second year—twelve years—neither I nor my brothers ate the food allotted to the governor. But the earlier governors—those preceding me—placed a heavy burden on the people and took forty shekels[a] of silver from them in addition to food and wine. Their assistants also lorded it over the people. But out of reverence for God I did not act like that."

Reflection: Nehemiah refused the food allowance and privileges that were rightfully his as governor. Instead, he lived sacrificially so that the people could be relieved of heavy burdens.

Leadership requires selflessness.

Jesus declared that the Son of Man came not to be served but to serve (Mark 10:45). Paul worked as a tentmaker so he would not be a burden to the churches he served (1 Thessalonians 2:9). Moses chose to suffer with his people rather than enjoy the momentary pleasures of Egypt (Hebrews 11:24-25). Sacrifice is at the heart of godly leadership.

In education, sacrifice might involve spending extra hours mentoring a struggling teacher, waiving personal convenience to ensure safety, or setting aside time for a student who needs guidance. Leaders who run their schedule with discipline know when to say yes to personal sacrifice for the sake of others.

Nehemiah shows us that sacrifice creates credibility. People will follow a leader who is willing to make sacrifices for their benefit.

Leadership Insight: Sacrifice builds credibility and trust in leadership.

Affirmation: *"I lead with a heart willing to sacrifice for others."*

Prayer: Lord, teach me to put the needs of others before my own comfort and to serve with joy.

Life Application: Identify one task or responsibility this week that would lighten the load for someone on your team. Step in quietly to serve them, demonstrating sacrificial leadership through action rather than words.

Life Application

Life Application

Day 18: Staying Focused Amid Distractions

Scripture: Nehemiah 6:3 (NIV)
"..so I sent messengers to them with this reply: "I am carrying on a great project and cannot go down. Why should the work stop while I leave it and go down to you?"

Reflection: When Sanballat and Geshem invited Nehemiah to meet with them, he refused, declaring, *"I am doing a great work and cannot come down."*

Focus is the mark of leaders who run their schedules with wisdom.

Jesus demonstrated this kind of focus when He declared that His food was to do the will of His Father (John 4:34). Paul wrote, *"This one thing I do: forgetting what is behind and straining toward what is ahead"* (Philippians 3:13). Leaders cannot allow distractions, criticism, or unnecessary obligations to pull them away from their actual assignment.

Distractions abound in schools. Endless meetings, reports, and minor conflicts can consume significant time and energy. But leaders who filter their schedule through the mission of student success will know when to say no. Running the schedule means protecting the work from constant interruptions.

Nehemiah's refusal to be sidetracked reminds us that sometimes the most powerful word a leader can say is "No."

Leadership Insight: Focus protects the mission from being weakened by distractions.

Affirmation: *"I protect my time and focus on what matters most."*

Prayer: Father, give me discernment to recognize distractions and courage to say no when needed.

Life Application: Write about one distraction that often pulls you away from your mission. How can you guard your focus this week?

Life Application

Life Application

Day 19: Praying for Strength

Scripture: Nehemiah 6:9 (NIV)
"They were all trying to frighten us, thinking, "Their hands will get too weak for the work, and it will not be completed." But I prayed, "Now strengthen my hands."

Reflection: Nehemiah's enemies tried to weaken his determination and resolve, but he prayed, *"Now strengthen my hands."* Disciplined leaders know that endurance requires God's strength, not just personal stamina. David often prayed for strength, declaring, *"The Lord is my strength and my shield"* (Psalm 28:7). Paul acknowledged his weakness but testified, *"When I am weak, then I am strong"* (2 Corinthians 12:10). Jesus Himself, in Gethsemane, prayed for strength to face the cross (Luke 22:42-44).

Leaders who admit their need for God's strength find renewal in His presence.

Discouragement and fatigue are common among school leaders. Leaders face criticism, long hours, and overwhelming expectations. But Godly reliance turns burdens into opportunities for God to show His power.

Nehemiah's short but powerful prayer reminds us that discipline in leadership includes returning again and again to God as the trustworthy source of strength.

Leadership Insight: Prayer sustains leaders with the strength they cannot produce on their own.

Affirmation: *"I draw daily strength from God to fulfill my leadership calling."*

Prayer: Lord, strengthen my hands and my heart for the work You have entrusted to me.

Life Application: Write a personal prayer asking God for strength in a specific area of your leadership.

Life Application

Life Application

Day 20: Celebrating Victories

Scripture: Nehemiah 6:15-16 (NIV)
"So the wall was completed on the twenty-fifth of Elul, in fifty-two days. When all our enemies heard about this, all the surrounding nations were afraid and lost their self-confidence, because they realized that this work had been done with the help of our God."

Reflection: When the wall was completed in fifty-two days, Nehemiah and the people celebrated. Their enemies recognized that the work had been done with God's help. Running your schedule with discipline also means pausing to celebrate victories.

God commanded Israel to hold feasts of remembrance so they would not forget His deliverance (Exodus 12:14). David often stopped to praise God in the midst of battles (Psalm 18). Jesus rejoiced with His disciples when they returned with reports of ministry success (Luke 10:20-21).

Celebration is not a waste of time; it is an act of worship that fuels future work.

Celebrating student achievement, teacher growth, or even small milestones builds morale and reinforces the mission. Leaders who stop to celebrate help their teams see progress instead of only pressure.

Nehemiah knew that acknowledging God's faithfulness was as crucial as laying stones. Leaders who discipline their schedule to include celebration create cultures of encouragement and gratitude.

Leadership Insight: Celebration fuels motivation and honors God's faithfulness.

Affirmation: *"I celebrate God's victories in my life and my school."*

Prayer: Thank You, Lord, for the victories You have given. Teach me to celebrate Your faithfulness and the progress of those I lead.

Life Application: Choose one recent victory in your school and celebrate it with your team this week — whether through a spoken word of thanks or a small gesture of appreciation.

Life Application

Life Application

Day 21: Leading with Integrity

Scripture: Nehemiah 7:2 (NIV)
"I put in charge of Jerusalem my brother Hanani, along with Hananiah the commander of the citadel, because he was a man of integrity and feared God more than most people do."

Reflection: Nehemiah appointed Hanani and Hananiah because of their integrity and reverence for God. He understood that leadership is not just about skill but about character. Integrity cannot be faked; it is either present or absent.

Leaders who avoid addressing lapses in integrity allow trust to erode.

Joseph demonstrated integrity in Potiphar's house when he refused temptation (Genesis 39:9). Samuel spoke at the end of his ministry and asked Israel if he had wronged anyone. They testified that he had not (1 Samuel 12:3-4). Jesus lived a blameless life and challenged the Pharisees' hypocrisy directly (Matthew 23:25-28). These examples remind us that integrity is the foundation of influence.

Leaders must be willing to have hard conversations when integrity is at stake—whether addressing dishonesty, unfair treatment, or a culture that tolerates mediocrity. Avoiding those conversations undermines credibility. Leaders' presence, courage, and clarity are required.

Nehemiah teaches us that leaders who value integrity appoint and develop others with the same standard. Difficult conversations are necessary to preserve the trust that leadership depends on.

Leadership Insight: Integrity gives leaders the credibility to correct mistakes and the courage to confront challenges.

Affirmation: *"I walk in integrity and hold others accountable to do the same."*

Prayer: Lord, let my life reflect Your character. Give me wisdom to address issues of integrity with grace and firmness.

Life Application: Write about one area where integrity must be strengthened in your school. How can you address it?

Life Application

Life Application

Weeks 4 and 5
Brave Presence: Showing up and Speaking up!

Day 22: Empowering Others

Scripture: Nehemiah 7:3-4 (NIV)
"I said to them, "The gates of Jerusalem are not to be opened until the sun is hot. While the gatekeepers are still on duty, have them shut the doors and bar them. Also appoint residents of Jerusalem as guards, some at their posts and some near their own houses." Now the city was large and spacious, but there were few people in it, and the houses had not yet been rebuilt."

Reflection: Nehemiah assigned gatekeepers, singers, and Levites to guard the city and serve the community. He empowered others by giving them real responsibility.

Leaders who avoid hard conversations often cling to control, but leaders who empower know when to release authority.

Moses shared his leadership burden with seventy elders, and God placed His Spirit on them (Numbers 11:16-17). Jesus sent out His disciples to heal and preach, entrusting them with His mission (Luke 9:1-2). Paul charged Timothy to entrust what he had received to faithful others (2 Timothy 2:2). Empowering is not about delegation alone—it is about accountability and trust.

At the school level, empowerment means equipping staff with clarity, support, and feedback. It sometimes requires conversations that clarify expectations or redirect practices. Avoiding those conversations stunts growth, but leaning into them creates development and capacity.

Nehemiah reminds us that empowerment is a combination of trust and accountability. Leaders who embrace hard conversations do so because they want people to succeed, not fail.

Leadership Insight: Empowerment grows when trust and accountability coexist.

Affirmation: *"I empower others with trust, clarity, and accountability."*

Prayer: Lord, give me courage to empower those around me with responsibility and wisdom to guide them well.

Life Application: Write about one person you need to empower more. What conversation will help them step into greater responsibility?

Life Application

Life Application

Day 23: Living with Accountability

Scripture: Nehemiah 8:1-3 (NIV)
"..all the people came together as one in the square before the Water Gate. They told Ezra the teacher of the Law to bring out the Book of the Law of Moses, which the Lord had commanded for Israel. So on the first day of the seventh month Ezra the priest brought the Law before the assembly, which was made up of men and women and all who were able to understand. He read it aloud from daybreak till noon as he faced the square before the Water Gate in the presence of the men, women and others who could understand. And all the people listened attentively to the Book of the Law."

Reflection: After the wall was rebuilt, the people gathered to hear Ezra read the Law aloud. This act of accountability reminded them that God's Word must shape the schedule of their lives. Joshua declared, *"As for me and my household, we will serve the Lord"* (Joshua 24:15). Paul emphasized discipline, saying he did not run aimlessly but kept his body in check so he would not be disqualified (1 Corinthians 9:24-27). Jesus taught openly, allowing His life to be examined by all (John 18:20).

Leaders who manage their time well know that accountability is not optional. Authentic leadership embraces accountability as a safeguard and a source of strength.

In schools, accountability comes through transparency, collaboration, and honest reflection. Leaders who open themselves to feedback model humility and integrity. This discipline creates cultures where growth is expected at every level.

Nehemiah's willingness to align the people under God's Word reminds us that disciplined leadership is not self-directed but God-directed.

Leadership Insight: Accountability strengthens discipline and keeps leaders aligned with God's mission.

Affirmation: *"I embrace accountability as a pathway to growth."*

Prayer: Lord, teach me to walk with integrity. Place mentors and colleagues in my life who will help me stay faithful to Your mission.

Life Application: Identify one person you trust to hold you accountable in your leadership. This week, have a face-to-face or phone conversation to invite them into that role and clarify how they can best support you.

Life Application

Life Application

Day 24: Joy in Obedience

Scripture: Nehemiah 8:10 (NIV)
"Nehemiah said, "Go and enjoy choice food and sweet drinks, and send some to those who have nothing prepared. This day is holy to our Lord. Do not grieve, for the joy of the Lord is your strength."

Reflection: After the reading of the Law, the people mourned. But Ezra and Nehemiah reminded them, *"The joy of the Lord is your strength."*

Leaders who are present with their people do not simply enforce rules. They remind them that joy and obedience go hand in hand.

Moses told Israel that obedience would bring blessing and life (Deuteronomy 30:19-20). Jesus taught His disciples that keeping His commands would lead to complete joy (John 15:10-11). Paul urged believers to rejoice always, even in difficulty (Philippians 4:4). Leadership presence means encouraging people to see that the work is not just a duty but a delight.

Leaders who are visible in classrooms, hallways, and community events bring encouragement and a reminder that the mission is worth celebrating. Their presence lifts morale and shows that the work matters. Joy is contagious, and leaders who walk with joy multiply strength among staff and students.

Leadership Insight: Presence combined with joy energizes people for the mission.

Affirmation: *"The joy of the Lord strengthens me and those I serve."*

Prayer: Lord, let my presence bring joy to those I lead. Remind me that obedience to You brings life and strength.

Life Application: Write down one way you can bring joy into your leadership presence this week.

Life Application

Life Application

Day 25: Confession and Renewal

Scripture: Nehemiah 9:2 (NIV)
"Those of Israelite descent had separated themselves from all foreigners. They stood in their places and confessed their sins and the sins of their ancestors.."

Reflection: The people confessed their sins publicly, separating themselves from what had hindered them. Nehemiah was present in that moment, walking with them through repentance and renewal.

Leaders must be willing to walk with their people through seasons of correction and growth.

Daniel confessed on behalf of his people, seeking God's mercy (Daniel 9:4-6). David declared, *"Create in me a pure heart, O God, and renew a steadfast spirit within me"* (Psalm 51:10). James urged believers to confess their sins to one another and to pray for healing (James 5:16). Leadership presence includes guiding people toward wholeness, not just achievement.

In schools, renewal may look like staff admitting when strategies are not working or students learning from mistakes. Leaders who walk with people in these moments demonstrate that growth comes from honesty and humility. This cultivates a safe environment where mistakes are not final but are stepping stones to maturity.

Leadership Insight: Presence in moments of repentance creates space for renewal and growth.

Affirmation: *"I walk with others through renewal and growth."*

Prayer: Lord, help me to model humility and create spaces where confession and growth can flourish.

Life Application: Take one tangible action this week to create an atmosphere of renewal in your school — such as starting a meeting with a word of encouragement, providing a brief moment of stillness, or surprising your staff with a small gesture of care.

Life Application

Life Application

Day 26: Remembering God's Faithfulness

Scripture: Nehemiah 9:6-8 (NIV)
"You alone are the Lord. You made the heavens, even the highest heavens, and all their starry host, the earth and all that is on it, the seas and all that is in them. You give life to everything, and the multitudes of heaven worship you. "You are the Lord God, who chose Abram and brought him out of Ur of the Chaldeans and named him Abraham. You found his heart faithful to you, and you made a covenant with him to give to his descendants the land of the Canaanites, Hittites, Amorites, Perizzites, Jebusites and Girgashites. You have kept your promise because you are righteous."

Reflection: As the people prayed, they recounted God's faithfulness through generations. Joshua set up memorial stones after crossing the Jordan so that future generations would remember God's deliverance (Joshua 4:6-7). David often rehearsed God's past faithfulness in the psalms (Psalm 77:11). Jesus reminded His disciples of miracles when their faith wavered (Mark 8:18-21). Presence in leadership includes calling attention to what God has already done.

Leaders who are present remind their teams of God's past victories, building confidence for the future.

In schools, this means reminding staff of student growth, past successes, and answered prayers. When leaders rehearse victories, they give perspective in seasons of challenge. People gain courage when they see that the God who worked before is still working now.

Leadership Insight: Leaders build faith by reminding their people of God's proven faithfulness.

Affirmation: *"I remember God's faithfulness and trust Him for the future."*

Prayer: Thank You, Lord, for Your faithfulness in the past. Remind me daily to encourage others with testimonies of Your goodness.

Life Application: Write down three ways God has shown faithfulness in your leadership this year.

Life Application

Life Application

Day 27: Renewing Commitments

Scripture: Nehemiah 10:29 (NIV)
"..all these now join their fellow Israelites the nobles, and bind themselves with a curse and an oath to follow the Law of God given through Moses the servant of God and to obey carefully all the commands, regulations and decrees of the Lord our Lord."

Reflection: The people renewed their covenant to walk in God's ways. Nehemiah's presence in this covenant moment shows us that leaders do not just call people to commitments; they walk with them in those commitments.

Joshua called Israel to choose whom they would serve, and declared, *"As for me and my house, we will serve the Lord"* (Joshua 24:15). Ezra renewed commitment through the reading of the Law. Jesus renewed His disciples' commitment after the resurrection, saying, *"Feed my sheep"* (John 21:17).

Renewal happens when leaders call people back to their "why."

Educationally, commitments include focusing on instructional priorities, strengthening relationships, or pursuing equity. Leaders who are present in these moments remind their staff and students that commitments are not one-time events but daily choices. Renewal requires reinforcement.

Leadership Insight: Presence during moments of recommitment strengthens resolve.

Affirmation: *"I renew my commitment to God's mission each day."*

Prayer: Lord, renew my commitment to Your calling and give me strength to lead others in theirs.

Life Application: Set aside five minutes this week to pray specifically over one area of your leadership where you feel weary. Ask God to renew your strength, restore your focus, and guide you with His wisdom.

Life Application

Life Application

Day 28: Stewardship of Resources

Scripture: Nehemiah 10:35-37 (NIV)
"We also assume responsibility for bringing to the house of the Lord each year the firstfruits of our crops and of every fruit tree. "As it is also written in the Law, we will bring the firstborn of our sons and of our cattle, of our herds and of our flocks to the house of our God, to the priests ministering there. "Moreover, we will bring to the storerooms of the house of our God, to the priests, the first of our ground meal, of our grain offerings, of the fruit of all our trees and of our new wine and olive oil. And we will bring a tithe of our crops to the Levites, for it is the Levites who collect the tithes in all the towns where we work."

Reflection: The people brought their firstfruits and tithes to ensure God's house was provided for. Nehemiah's presence reinforced the importance of stewardship.

Leaders who are present demonstrate wise use of resources.

Joseph modeled stewardship by preparing Egypt for famine (Genesis 41:48-49). David organized the resources for Solomon to build the temple (1 Chronicles 29:2-3). Jesus praised the widow who gave her all, showing that stewardship is measured by faithfulness, not amount (Mark 12:41-44).

Stewardship is visible in how time, finances, and human resources are used. Leaders who are present ensure resources are aligned with what benefits students most. Wise stewardship builds trust and demonstrates integrity.

Leadership Insight: Stewardship of resources demonstrates faithfulness to God's mission and to the people served.

Affirmation: *"I am a faithful steward of all God has entrusted to me."*

Prayer: Lord, help me to wisely steward the time, resources, and people You have placed in my care.

Life Application: Choose one habit this week to guard your time or resources and practice it every day.

Life Application

Life Application

Day 29: Guarding Against Compromise

Scripture: Nehemiah 13:11 (NIV)
"So I rebuked the officials and asked them, "Why is the house of God neglected?" Then I called them together and stationed them at their posts."

Reflection: When Nehemiah returned to Jerusalem and saw that the Levites had been neglected, he confronted the leaders and corrected the issue.

Leaders who are present notice when compromise has crept in.

Phinehas acted swiftly to remove sin from Israel and turned God's anger away (Numbers 25:11). Elijah confronted Israel for wavering between two opinions, calling them back to God (1 Kings 18:21). Jesus cleansed the temple, driving out those who turned worship into profit (Matthew 21:12-13). Presence is not passive. It demands vigilance and courage to confront compromise.

In schools, compromise may look like lowering expectations, ignoring inequities, or tolerating an unhealthy culture. Leaders who are present notice these cracks and take steps to restore integrity. Protecting the mission requires the courage to confront, not simply observe.

Leadership Insight: Presence requires vigilance to guard against compromising one's values.

Affirmation: *"I protect the mission by standing firm in truth."*

Prayer: Lord, give me courage to confront compromise with wisdom and grace.

Life Application: Identify one area where compromise may have entered your leadership or school. Take a step this week to address it with integrity and clarity.

Life Application

Life Application

Day 30: Trusting God with the Future

Scripture: Nehemiah 13:31 (NIV)
"I also made provision for contributions of wood at designated times, and for the firstfruits. Remember me with favor, my God."

Reflection: Nehemiah's final recorded words were, *"Remember me with favor, my God."* He recognized that his leadership and legacy were ultimately in God's hands.

Leaders who are present know that while they work faithfully, the future belongs to God.

Moses entrusted Israel to Joshua, knowing God would guide them (Deuteronomy 31:7-8). David prepared Solomon but reminded him to walk in God's ways (1 Kings 2:2-3). Jesus entrusted His disciples with the Great Commission and promised to be with them always (Matthew 28:19-20). Leaders who trust God with the future lead with peace rather than anxiety.

As school leaders, we plant seeds that we may never see grow to a complete harvest. Leaders who stay present today while trusting God for tomorrow provide stability and hope for their staff and students. Our presence in the moment is part of the legacy God is writing.

Leadership Insight: Presence today builds faith for tomorrow, knowing the future rests in God's hands.

Affirmation: *"I trust God with my future and the legacy of my leadership."*

Prayer: Lord, help me to be fully present today and trust You with what lies ahead.

Life Application: Take a short walk through your school this week. As you walk, silently pray over the classrooms, students, and staff, asking God to cover the future with His guidance.

Life Application

Life Application

Day 31: Finishing Well

Scripture: 2 Timothy 4:7 (NIV)
"I have fought the good fight, I have finished the race, I have kept the faith."

Reflection: Paul declared, *"I have fought the good fight, I have finished the race, I have kept the faith."* Nehemiah, too, finished his assignment, leaving Jerusalem secured with rebuilt walls, renewed worship, and reformed practices.

> ***Leaders who finish well do not avoid hard conversations. They face them, knowing the health of the mission depends on it.***

Jesus cried out on the cross, *"It is finished"* (John 19:30). His willingness to confront sin directly gave us eternal life. Joshua led Israel faithfully until his final words of covenant renewal (Joshua 24:14-15). Leaders who finish strong remain faithful to their calling to the end, not avoiding brutal truths along the way.

In schools, finishing well may look like addressing unresolved issues, speaking difficult truths with love, or ensuring systems are in place for sustainable success after you are gone. A leader's legacy is not measured by how easy they made the journey, but by how faithfully they completed their mission.

Nehemiah's story closes with a reminder that leadership is temporary, but God's mission is eternal. Leaders who embrace this truth confront what must be faced and finish their race with faith intact.

Leadership Insight: Finishing well requires courage, honesty, and faithfulness until the end.

Affirmation: *"I will finish the race with integrity and courage."*

Prayer: Father, give me endurance to finish well. Help me to lead with courage, honesty, and faithfulness until the end of my assignment.

Life Application: Write about the legacy you want to leave as a leader. What conversations must you have now to finish well?

Life Application

Life Application

About the Author

Dr. Tenry D. Berry is a lifelong educator, leader, and developer of people. Born and raised in Valdosta, Georgia, he is the eldest son of the late Henry and Patricia Berry. A graduate of Valdosta High School, Dr. Berry continued his academic journey at Valdosta State University, earning a Bachelor of Science in Education in 2003, before completing a Master's degree, an Educational Specialist, and later a Doctorate in Educational Leadership — all achieved with excellence, perseverance, and an unwavering commitment to growth from Nova Southeastern University.

With more than two decades in education, Dr. Berry has served as a teacher, mentor, principal, and district leader. He now serves as the Assistant Superintendent of Lowndes County Schools, where he leads with vision, compassion, and a passion for developing leaders, strengthening instructional practices, and cultivating environments where students and educators thrive. His work is grounded in mentorship, equity, data-informed decision-making, and a deep belief that every student has limitless potential.

Beyond the school system, Dr. Berry is an instructor at the collegiate level and an active ministry leader. He currently serves on staff as a Director at Kingdom Impact Center in Valdosta, GA. His ministry work reflects his heart for people, discipleship, and spiritual development. Above all accomplishments, Dr. Berry treasures his relationship with God and his family. He is joyfully married to Paige, and together they are raising three incredible children — Kendahl, Khloe, and Kingston.

This book reflects the core of who he is — a teacher, builder of leaders, encourager of purpose, and a man committed to helping others grow spiritually, mentally, and personally. Through these pages, Dr. Berry invites readers into wisdom, reflection, and transformation as they walk out their God-given call.

www.ingramcontent.com/pod-product-compliance
Lightning Source LLC
Chambersburg PA
CBHW072146160426
43197CB00012B/2267